Di_____ the Zoo

Based on *The Terrible Accident*
written by Celia Warren

Illustrated by Derek Brazell

Adapted by Sally Carpenter for the
Heinemann English Readers series

Heinemann Educational Publishers
Halley Court, Jordan Hill, Oxford OX2 8EJ

An imprint of Harcourt Education Limited
Heinemann is a registered trademark of Harcourt Education Limited.

Literacy World Satellites edition © Celia Warren 2000
Heinemann English Readers edition © Celia Warren, Harcourt Education Limited
2006

10 09 08 07 06
10 9 8 7 6 5 4 3 2 1

British Library Cataloguing in Publication Data is available from the British Library
on request.

ISBN 0435 294717 / 978 0435 294717

Copyright notice
All rights reserved. No part of this publication may be reproduced in any form or
by any means (including photocopying or storing it in any medium by electronic
means and whether or not transiently or incidentally to some other use of this
publication) without the written permission of the copyright owner, except in
accordance with the provisions of the Copyright, Designs and Patents Act 1988 or
under the terms of a licence issued by the Copyright Licensing Agency, 90
Tottenham Court Road, London W1T 4LP. Applications for the copyright owner's
written permission should be addressed to the publisher.

Designed by Nicola Kenwood @ Hakoona Matata Designs
Illustrated by Derek Brazell

Cover design by Nicola Kenwood @ Hakoona Matata Designs

Printed and bound in Malaysia by Vivar

Acknowledgements
Every effort has been made to contact copyright holders of material reproduced
in this book. Any omissions will be rectified in subsequent printings if notice is
given to the publishers.

Contents

Key words 4

Disaster at the Zoo 6

Activities 20

Notes for teachers and parents 23

Answers 24

Key words

zoo

zookeeper

gorilla

elephant

gorilla pit

railings

Joe   Lucy   Dad   Mum

Disaster at the Zoo

Many children like going to the zoo. It is a safe way to see wild animals. But accidents *can* happen.

Joe and Lucy went to the zoo with their Mum and Dad. Lucy was Joe's little sister. She was only two. Joe helped to look after her.

to go
We are going to the zoo. They went to the zoo.

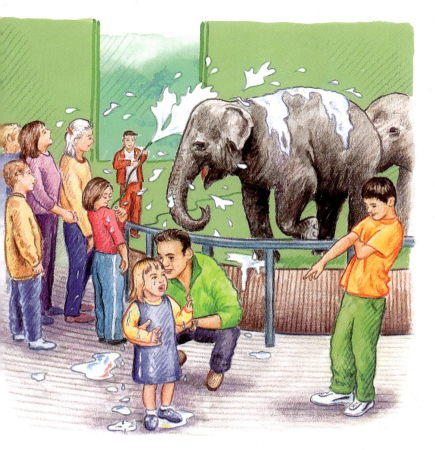

Joe wanted to see the elephants first. The elephants were having a bath. Lucy ran too near the water and got wet. Joe laughed but Lucy began to cry.

'Don't laugh at her,' said Dad. 'Be nice to your sister.'

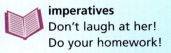

imperatives
Don't laugh at her!
Do your homework!

Next, Mum bought them each an ice cream. Lucy dropped her ice cream on the ground. Joe laughed, but Lucy began to cry.

'Don't laugh at her,' said Mum. 'You should look after your sister.'

her / his
She dropped her ice cream. He laughed at his sister.

Then Lucy wanted to see the gorillas. There were two female gorillas. One held a baby gorilla in her arms.

There was a big male gorilla too. His name was Buster. He was sleeping under a tree.

was / were
He was sleeping. They were sleeping.
I was laughing. We were laughing.

Everyone wanted to see the gorillas. They all tried to push to the front.

'Help your sister, Joe,' said Dad. 'She's very little.'

So Joe took hold of Lucy's hand and pushed his way to the front. But the gorillas were down in a pit. Lucy could not see them.

pit: a big, deep hole

'I want to see the gorillas!' cried Lucy.
So Joe helped her to stand on the wall and Lucy looked down into the pit. Joe turned round to look for Mum and Dad. They would be pleased that he was helping Lucy.

 past simple tense
He turned round.
She looked down.

But, just then, Lucy climbed over the railings.

'Joe!' shouted Dad. 'Grab her!'

But it was too late for Joe to catch her. Lucy slipped right down into the gorilla pit. Everyone started screaming and shouting.

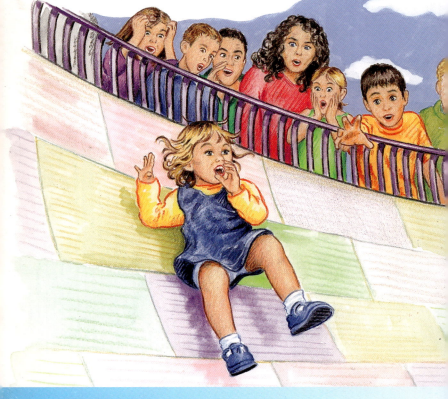

to slip: to slide and fall
to grab: to catch

Joe pushed his way quickly through the shouting people. All he could think of was getting to Lucy.

A zookeeper was running into the gorilla pit. Joe ran in after him.

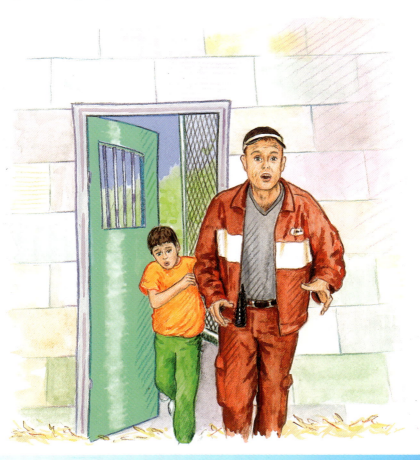

past continuous tense
He was running.
They were shouting.

Then, suddenly, the zookeeper stopped running. He stood very still.

'Oh no!' he said. Joe stood still too. He looked at the gorillas. One of the females was holding the baby gorilla. The other female gorilla was holding Lucy!

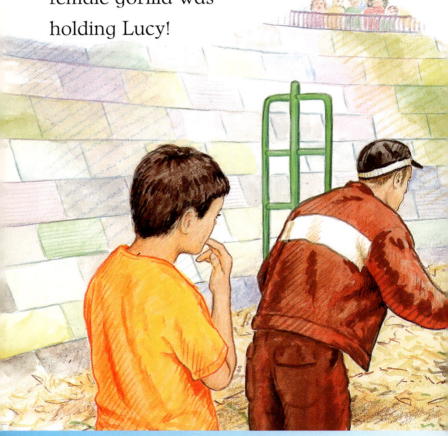

to stand still: to stand without moving

The crowd became very quiet. Everyone stood still. Lucy was very frightened but she was not crying.

Slowly the zookeeper crept closer to the female gorilla. Joe kept close behind the zookeeper. Buster, the big male, was still asleep under the tree.

opposites
big/small   male/female

But then Buster woke up! When he saw the zookeeper in the pit, he beat his chest and bared his teeth. Then the zookeeper saw Joe.

'What are you doing in here?' he shouted. 'Get out! It's dangerous!'

Just then Joe and the zookeeper watched in horror as Buster went over to the female gorilla and grabbed Lucy!

'Joe!' screamed Lucy.

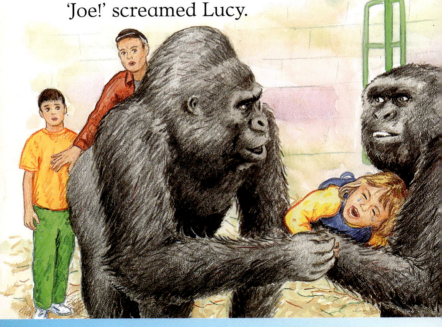

to beat your chest: to hit your chest with your fists to show anger
to bare your teeth: to show your teeth

Joe was very frightened. He did not know what to do.

The zookeeper tried to get near Buster, but Buster bared his teeth again.

'Joe!' cried Lucy, as she held out her arms.

Then Joe walked slowly up to Buster and held out his arms too.

opposites
slowly/quickly   sadly/happily

Buster and Joe looked at each other. Lucy still held out her arms to Joe. Joe held out his arms too. He kept looking at Buster's face. Then slowly Buster handed Lucy over to Joe!

Joe held Lucy tightly in his arms. Buster looked at Joe and Lucy. Then he turned towards the other gorillas. He jumped onto his swing as if nothing had happened.

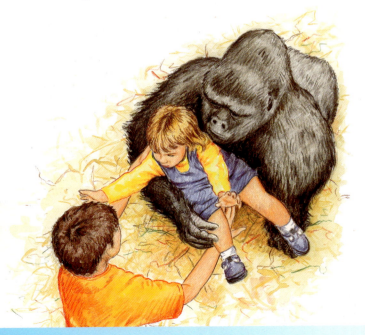

He kept looking.
He carried on looking. He continued looking.

Quickly, the zookeeper hurried Joe and Lucy out of the gorilla pit. Mum and Dad were waiting outside. They gave Lucy and Joe a big hug.

'Well done, Joe,' said Dad. 'You saved Lucy's life.'

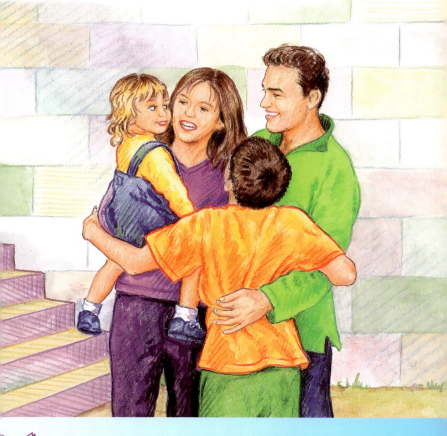

 to hurry someone: to make someone do something quickly
to give someone a hug: put your arms round someone

Read and remember

Are these sentences true (T) or false (F)? Correct the false ones. (In some of the activities that follow, the first question has been done to help you.)

1 Lucy was three. (*F. Lucy was two.*)
2 Joe was Lucy's brother.
3 Joe wanted to see the gorillas first.
4 Lucy dropped her ice cream.
5 The female gorilla was called Buster.
6 Lucy climbed over the railings.
7 Lucy slipped into the gorilla pit.
8 The zookeeper saved Lucy.

Put these sentences in the correct order.

a The zookeeper ran into the gorilla pit.
b Lucy slipped into the gorilla pit.
c Buster gave Lucy to Joe.
d Joe held out his arms.
e Joe ran after the zookeeper.
f Mum, Dad, Lucy and Joe went to see the gorillas. *(1)*
g Joe helped Lucy to stand on the wall.
h Buster grabbed Lucy from the female gorilla.

In the past

Complete these sentences using the past simple verbs in the box.

| tried | was | went | turned | ran | were |
| gave | watched | walked | wanted | shouted |

1 Yesterday I *went* to the park with my friends.

2 He _____ ten.

3 Mum _____ to see the baby animals.

4 They _____ frightened of the big animals.

5 During the soccer match, she _____ to kick the ball.

6 He _____ to climb over the wall.

7 Someone _____ and I _____ round.

8 Last night we _____ a TV program about wild animals.

9 We _____ to the zoo.

10 I _____ Dad a book for his birthday.

Now make up five sentences of your own using past simple verbs.

Imperatives

An imperative is a command or an instruction. Match each imperative to a picture.

1. Help me!
2. Stop!
3. Don't look at my book.
4. Don't laugh at me!
5. Wake up!
6. Get out!

Notes for teachers and parents

Background

1 A gorilla is an ape. Can the students name any other apes (examples: chimpanzee, orang-utan)? Where are they found? Students can find out more about chimpanzees by reading the HER book **Jane Goodall: Living with the Chimpanzees**.

2 Joe's parents expected him to look after his little sister. What do the students think about this? Should older children always look after their younger brothers and sisters?

3 The zookeeper was angry with Joe because Joe ran into the gorilla pit. What else do the students think that Joe could have done?

4 What do the students think about keeping animals in zoos? Are there any animals which should not be kept in zoos? Why?

How to get the most out of this book

1 It is helpful if the students can read the book in pairs, reading one page aloud each. Reading aloud will hep the students remember the words.

2 Encourage the students to look at the key words pages before reading the rest of the book. These pages are designed to be used as a picture glossary. It is also helpful to have an English dictionary available for the students to use.

3 The coloured strips at the bottom of each page show the language used in the text in either a different way or a different context, or may help introduce a new word. Looking at these will help the students to better understand the text and to develop their English.

Answers

Read and remember

Are these sentences true (T) or false (F)? Correct the false ones.
1 F. Lucy was two.
2 T.
3 F. Joe wanted to see the elephants first.
4 T.
5 F. The male gorilla was called Buster.
6 T.
7 T.
8 F. Joe saved Lucy.

Put these sentences in the correct order.
1 f
2 g
3 b
4 a
5 e
6 h
7 d
8 c

In the past
1 went
2 was
3 wanted
4 were
5 ran
6 tried
7 shouted, turned
8 watched
9 walked
10 gave

Imperatives
1 b
2 d
3 f
4 a
5 e
6 c

24